WAITING FOR GOD

8 STUDIES FOR INDIVIDUALS OR GROUPS

Juanita Ryan

With Notes for Leaders

IVP Connect

An imprint of InterVarsity Press
Downers Grove, Illinois

InterVarsity Press
P.O. Box 1400, Downers Grove, IL 60515-1426
World Wide Web: www.ivpress.com
E-mail: email@ivpress.com

InterVarsity Press® is the book-publishing division of InterVarsity Christian Fellowship/USA®, a
movement of students and faculty active on campus at hundreds of universities, colleges and schools
of nursing in the United States of America, and a member movement of the International Fellowship
of Evangelical Students. For information about local and regional activities, write Public Relations
Dept., InterVarsity Christian Fellowship/USA, 6400 Schroeder Rd., P.O. Box 7895, Madison, WI
53707-7895, or visit the IVCF website at <www.intervarsity.org>.

LifeGuide® is a registered trademark of InterVarsity Christian Fellowship.

Design: Cindy Kiple

Cover image: © Tatiana Ivanova/Dreamstime.com

ISBN 978-0-8308-3146-3

Printed in the United States of America ∞

 InterVarsity Press is committed to protecting the environment and to the responsible
use of natural resources. As a member of Green Press Initiative we use recycled paper
whenever possible. To learn more about the Green Press Initiative, visit <www
.greenpressinitiative.org>.

P   20   19   18   17   16   15   14   13   12   11   10   9   8   7   6   5   4   3   2

Y   30   29   28   27   26   25   24   23   22   21   20   19   18   17   16   15   14

Contents

Getting the Most Out of
Waiting for God

"How long, O God, how long? Will you forget me forever?" This was the cry of the psalmist. It was the cry of many of the prophets. It may also be the cry of your heart at this time in your life. Or it may be that you endured such a time in your past and are left with questions about it. Maybe you also know someone who is going through such a time.

We will all experience times of waiting in the midst of uncertainty or suffering or great need. During these times we may feel desperate for something to change or for a sign of hope that things will change soon. But often in our periods of waiting, nothing happens, nothing changes. If anything, things seem to get worse.

In the midst of such waiting it can seem like God is silent. We might fear that God has forgotten us and feel too discouraged to even turn to God for help. Or we may turn to God only to become more frightened and dismayed because our prayers for help or deliverance seem to go unanswered.

Not all waiting is painful. Sometimes waiting is a time of great anticipation outwardly, such as when we're planning a wedding, expecting a new child in the family, or preparing for an exciting change of job or location. But even these happier times of waiting can be full of anxieties. We may fear that something will go terribly wrong. Or that we are making the wrong decision. Or that we will not be adequate for the task. Or that we will not have the emotional or social skills to weather the adaptation. These fears are often hidden, sometimes even from ourselves, but they can make even times of excited waiting very difficult. And again we may find inwardly that we are having trouble trusting God to protect and provide for us.

How is it possible to meet God in our times of waiting? How do we meet God when God seems unresponsive to our desperate need?

The God of the Bible is the God who has promised to always be with us. Always. Even in our times of waiting. Even when our situation is desperate or our heart is full of anxiety. Even when we believe God is silent or unresponsive to our need or inattentive to our future. Even when we feel like we have lost all faith.

The following studies are designed to help you give voice to your distress and gain perspective on your fears in times of waiting, and to open your heart and mind to the One who is with you always.

Suggestions for Individual Study

1. As you begin each study, pray that God will speak to you through his Word.

2. Read the introduction to the study and respond to the personal reflection question or exercise. This is designed to help you focus on God and on the theme of the study.

3. Each study deals with a particular passage so that you can delve into the author's meaning in that context. Read and reread the passage to be studied. The questions are written using the language of the New International Version, so you may wish to use that version of the Bible. The New Revised Standard Version is also recommended.

4. This is an inductive Bible study, designed to help you discover for yourself what Scripture is saying. The study includes three types of questions. Observation questions ask about the basic facts: who, what, when, where and how. Interpretation questions delve into the meaning of the passage. Application questions help you discover the implications of the text for growing in Christ. These three keys unlock the treasures of Scripture. Write your answers to the questions in the spaces provided or in a personal journal. Writing can bring clarity and deeper understanding of yourself and of God's Word.

5. It might be good to have a Bible dictionary handy. Use it to look up any unfamiliar words, names or places.

6. Use the prayer suggestion to guide you in thanking God for what you have learned and to pray about the applications that have come to mind.

7. You may want to go on to the suggestion under "Now or Later," or you may want to use that idea for your next study.

Suggestions for Members of a Group Study

1. Come to the study prepared. Follow the suggestions for individual study mentioned above. You will find that careful preparation will greatly enrich your time spent in group discussion.

2. Be willing to participate in the discussion. The leader of your group will not be lecturing. Instead, he or she will be encouraging the members of the group to discuss what they have learned. The leader will be asking the questions that are found in this guide.

3. Stick to the topic being discussed. Your answers should be based on the verses which are the focus of the discussion and not on outside authorities such as commentaries or speakers. These studies focus on a particular passage of Scripture. Only rarely should you refer to other portions of the Bible. This allows for everyone to participate in in-depth study on equal ground.

4. Be sensitive to the other members of the group. Listen attentively when they describe what they have learned. You may be surprised by their insights! Each question assumes a variety of answers. Many questions do not have "right" answers, particularly questions that aim at meaning or application. Instead the questions push us to explore the passage more thoroughly.

When possible, link what you say to the comments of others. Also, be affirming whenever you can. This will encourage some of the more hesitant members of the group to participate.

5. Be careful not to dominate the discussion. We are sometimes so eager to express our thoughts that we leave too little opportunity for others to respond. By all means participate! But allow others to also.

6. Expect God to teach you through the passage being discussed and through the other members of the group. Pray that you will have an enjoyable and profitable time together, but also that as a result of the study you will find ways that you can take action individually and/or as a group.

7. Remember that anything said in the group is considered confidential and should not be discussed outside the group unless specific permission is given to do so.

8. If you are the group leader, you will find additional suggestions at the back of the guide.

1

When Waiting Is Difficult

Psalm 13

We do not like to wait. Whether it is being put on hold on the phone or standing in a long line at the store, waiting irritates us.

Sometimes, though, waiting is more than an annoyance. Sometimes it's torturous. Waiting for a loved one to come out of surgery. Waiting for the results of a biopsy taken to test for cancer. Waiting for an answer to a prayer we have been praying for months or even years. This kind of waiting is difficult because it is full of fear. We are left in these times with terrible questions about our future—and terrible questions about God.

Scripture testifies to these times of painful waiting, putting into words our anguished fears. Wonderfully, Scripture also offers us hope and strength for these times of difficult waiting.

GROUP DISCUSSION. What kinds of situations are hardest for you to wait patiently in? Why?

PERSONAL REFLECTION. Think of a time when you waited a long time for an answer to prayer. What anxieties did you experience while waiting? How did this time of waiting affect your sense of God's presence with you?

In this psalm, the psalmist voices the great distress he is experiencing in a time of waiting. In doing so, he offers us permission and language to express our struggles to God. *Read Psalm 13.*

---

1. How would you title each of the three sections of this psalm (vv. 1-2, vv. 3-4 and vv. 5-6)?

---

2. What do we learn from the first section (vv. 1-2) about how waiting affects the psalmist mentally and emotionally?

---

3. How does the experience of waiting affect how he experiences God (v. 1)?

---

4. How does the psalmist's mental, emotional and spiritual experience while waiting compare with your experiences during times of difficult waiting?

5. What does the psalmist ask for in verse 3?

6. What is the psalmist convinced will happen if God doesn't answer him (v. 4)?

7. What does the psalmist commit to doing in the final section of the psalm?

8. What does he reaffirm about God?

9. How might remembering these truths about God help you when waiting is difficult?

10. How can this text be a resource to you in your times of waiting?

---

11. In a time of quiet join the psalmist in his prayer found in verse 3: "Look on me and answer, LORD my God." Sit in silence before God, perhaps with your hands open on your lap, with this prayer in your heart. Share or write about your experience in this time of quiet before God.

Express your longing to know God's presence with you in whatever difficulty or challenge you are facing.

Now or Later

Using Psalm 13 as a model, journal a prayer. Express to God whatever difficulty you are experiencing. Ask for God's help and for the faith to trust that God is with you. Reaffirm what you know to be true about who God is.

2

Wisdom in Waiting

Waiting often causes anxiety. We plead with God to hurry and act even while we battle a growing fear that God has deserted us. To cope, we may try to take control of things that we have no ability to control, often causing harm to ourselves or others. We can become demanding and manipulative in attempts to make things go the way we think they ought to go. And when our attempts fail, anger may take hold and lead us to say and do things that are hurtful. The end result will likely be exhaustion and despair.

Wisdom teaches another way: wait for God to lead, for God to guide, for God to act. Rather than relying on ourselves to try to control things that are out of our control, wisdom calls us to depend on God. Rather than relying on our very limited understanding, wisdom instructs us to trust God's omniscience and goodness. In times of waiting we are invited to choose wisdom, to ask for deeper trust in, and deeper surrender to, the One who loves us and longs to show us the way.

GROUP DISCUSSION. Imagine you're giving a friend, a daughter or son, or a grandchild instruction in three or four key points of wisdom for life. What would you say?

PERSONAL REFLECTION. Think of a time of waiting in your life.

What wisdom did you receive from God during that time?

Our text—words on living wisely from a loving father to his son—teaches us to choose wisdom in our waiting by "[trusting] in the Lord with all [our] heart" rather than placing our confidence in our own abilities. *Read Proverbs 3:1-12.*

---

1. List all that the father advises the son to do.

---

2. What benefits does the father say will come from following this wisdom?

---

3. What reactions might a son have to hearing these instructions on wisdom?

---

4. What might it mean to "bind [love and faithfulness] around your neck" and to "write them on the tablet of your heart" (v. 3)?

(Ver.1)   Matt. 16, 18-19   EPH. 6:17

3 Kinds of words'' Written Word

(2) logos - living word we have understanding Heb. 4:12-13

(3) rama - unseen 1 John 3:9 1 John 1:8-10, 2:1-2(a) 3:4,9

5. What does it mean to "trust in the LORD with all your heart" (v. 5)?

6. What might it mean for a person to acknowledge God in all their ways (v. 6)?

7. Which of the instructions listed are difficult for you to follow?

What makes those particular instructions difficult?

8. Which of these instructions speaks to you the most at this time in your life?

9. Spend a few minutes contemplating the list you made in response to question one. Ask God to remind you of ways you are following the instructions in Proverbs 3. Write what comes to your mind.

10. Ask God to show you where God would have you change. Write your response to what it seems God is saying to you.

_____

11. How might these instructions be especially important for you in times of waiting?

_____

12. How might following this wisdom lead to a greater sense of God's presence with you?

Thank God for the privilege of relying on God and God's wisdom in all you do.

Now or Later

Focus on one or two of the instructions from this text this week. Each day put it into practice. Make a journal entry at the end of each day about the impact that following this wisdom had on your day.

3

Waiting for God

In times of waiting, our focus is often on future events. We wonder what will happen next. We wonder if the changes we hope for will ever come.

But there is more going on in our minds and hearts in times of waiting; there's something more that we are waiting for. Our greatest need and longing in times of waiting (and in all times) is for God. When we quiet ourselves during these times, this deeper experience of waiting begins to emerge.

> Something happens to us in this kind of waiting. We are brought to attention. Our hearts and minds and spirits focus on what matters most, on what is most real, on our deepest longings for God.
>
> When we wait as if we are watching for our soul's true love to appear, we find that the focus of our waiting is not so much about the future as it is about this present moment. This moment we can be right here, right now with our need, with our hunger, with our thirst for the One who is our Home, our Hope, our Help.[*]

This kind of waiting is what the psalmist gives voice to in Psalm 42.

GROUP DISCUSSION. Reflect on a time when you were separated from someone you love. What was the experience of that separation like for you? How would you describe the experience of being reunited with this loved one?

PERSONAL REFLECTION. Think about the idea of God being your "soul's true love." Do you tend to view and relate to God that way? Why or why not?

In this text the psalmist struggles to hang on to hope, giving voice to an experience that is often a part of waiting for all of us. *Read Psalm 42.*

1. What words and images does the psalmist use to describe his emotional, physical and spiritual experience of waiting for and longing for God?

2. Why do you think the experience of feeling separated from God creates so much distress for the psalmist?

3. Given the descriptions of what it can be like to wait for and long for God, how difficult is it, in your experience, to stay aware of these deep feelings when you're in the middle of a season of waiting?

4. What value might there be in staying aware of these feelings and even giving voice to them?

_____

5. Which of the psalmist's descriptions of longing for God do you most relate to?

_____

6. What were men saying to the psalmist about God?

How do you think their words added to the psalmist's distress?

_____

7. What contrast does the psalmist draw in verses 3 and 4 between what he remembers and what he is currently experiencing?

_____

8. What truths does the psalmist return to in order to encourage himself in this time of waiting and longing for a sense of God's presence?

9. What truths and experiences of God do you find yourself returning to in times of waiting and longing for a sense of God's presence?

---

10. What does the psalmist say in verse 8 that God is doing for him even through this time of waiting?

---

11. What can you see God doing in you and for you in your own time of waiting?

Express your longing for God directly to God.

Now or Later

Read the first two verses of this psalm and sit quietly in openness to God for two or three minutes. Repeat this three more times. Write about whatever you experienced in this time.

---

*Juanita Ryan, *Keep Breathing: What to Do When You Can't Figure Out What to Do* (Seattle: CreateSpace, 2009), p. 102.

4

Waiting Together

Job 2:11-13; 6:1-17; 13:1-5

Times of waiting can be very difficult. But waiting with the support of others can literally make an unbearable situation bearable. One of the ways that God is present to us in times of waiting is through the compassion, kindness and respectfulness of others; they minister the loving presence of God to us.

In his book *The View from the Hearse,* Joseph Bayly describes an experience with a friend who was not able to be supportive to him and a friend who was:

> I was sitting, torn by grief. Someone came and talked to me of God's dealings, of why it happened, of hope beyond the grave. He talked constantly, he said things I knew were true. I was unmoved, except to wish he'd go away. He finally did.
>
> Another came and sat beside me. He didn't talk. He didn't ask leading questions. He just sat beside me for an hour and more, listened when I said something, answered briefly, prayed simply, left. I was moved. I was comforted. I hated to see him go.*

The friend who made a positive difference was the one who was fully present to him in his pain. Friends like that are a true gift in the midst of our times of waiting.

GROUP DISCUSSION. When have you seen well-meaning "support" cause more pain and hurt instead of helping someone? Where did the person offering support go wrong?

PERSONAL REFLECTION. Imagine yourself waiting by yourself for a friend or family member to go through surgery. What thoughts and feelings come to you as you picture this? Now imagine yourself waiting with a supportive friend. What would you want from your friend? What would it feel like to receive that from your friend?

Job's experience of friends who sat with him in his time of waiting for God to answer his heart's cry can both encourage and instruct us. At first these friends were truly present with Job, but they then began to withdraw from him and his pain, offering unwanted advice and criticism. *Read Job 2:11-13; 6:1-17; 13:1-5.*

1. Job has suffered unspeakable losses. When his friends come to visit him, what is their initial response (2:11-13)?

2. What did these friends communicate to Job through that initial response (2:11-13)?

3. After some time, Job speaks in anguish (Job 3), and his friends begin to offer advice and correction. What is Job's response to them (6:1-3, 14-17; 13:1-5)?

4. What do you think Job is asking of his friends in verse 6:14?

5. In Job 13:1-5 Job states that his friends' silence was much wiser than their words. Why is this so often true in times of great anguish?

6. Why is it sometimes difficult to listen in silent empathy and compassion to a friend's "impetuous" words that seem to indicate a "forsaking of the fear of the Almighty"?

7. What does it feel like to be the one receiving the gifts of silent empathy and compassion from others while we wait?

8. How do you offer the kind of support Job was asking for to your friends? Think of specific examples of times you have offered or could offer this kind of support.

9. How do your friends offer you this kind of support? Think of specific examples.

10. How might this kind of support from a friend help you to experience God in times of waiting?

11. In what situation in your life right now could you use support from a friend?

Pray for your friends, thanking God for the gifts of help and support you each receive from the other.

Now or Later

Spend some time with a friend this week, listening with compassion and respect to whatever they are going through and inviting them to do the same for you.

---

*Joseph Bayly, *The View from the Hearse* (New York: New Family Library, 1972), pp. 40-41.

5

Waiting with Hope

The Gospel of Luke begins with the story of a promise within a promise. In the opening scene we meet a man named Zechariah who has been waiting for many years with his wife to be blessed with a child. He and his wife have also been waiting, along with all the people of Israel, for the promised Messiah.

Luke recounts how an angel comes to Zechariah and announces to him that what he has been waiting for is about to happen. He and his wife will have a son. And that son will prepare the way for the coming of the Messiah.

But the waiting has been long, and it is not easy to wait with hope. Over time hope tends to dim and discouragement, doubt and even despair begin to set in. By the time the angel appears to Zechariah, he has all but given up. The message is almost too much to grasp, too much to hope for; he expresses doubt that the events will actually come to pass.

But as the story unfolds we are reminded again that our hope is in God—God who is lovingly, powerfully active in our lives, in our story, in history.

GROUP DISCUSSION. How would you define hope?

PERSONAL REFLECTION. Why is it sometimes so difficult to hang on to hope in times of waiting?

In the text for this study we listen in as an angel tells Zechariah that his time of waiting is about to become a time of receiving. And we watch as Zechariah struggles to hope. *Read Luke 1:1-25, 57-80.*

1. What title would you give to the first section of this text (vv. 1-25)?

What title would you give to the second section (vv. 57-80)?

2. Elizabeth and Zechariah had been praying and waiting for a child for decades. They had probably given up all hope. The nation of Israel had been waiting for the promised Messiah for hundreds of years and may have been struggling to hang on to hope. In what way can you relate to this kind of experience?

3. Put yourself in Zechariah's place. What do you imagine he is experiencing during his encounter with the angel?

4. How might the "sign" of being temporarily mute have been a gift to Zechariah in his time of waiting for their son to be born?

5. What does the angel say that the promised son will do to prepare people for the coming of the Messiah (v. 17)?

6. What does Zechariah say that his son will do to prepare people for the Lord (vv. 76-77)?

7. Which of these preparations for receiving more of God might God be doing in your life at this time?

8. How have you seen God prepare you for gifts from God that you've been waiting for?

9. The two primary human actors in this story are Zechariah and his wife, Elizabeth. But the primary Actor in this story is clearly God. Take a few minutes to reread the story with this perspective in mind. How does this perspective change how you see this story?

_____

10. How does seeing God as the major Actor in this story change how you see your own story?

_____

11. Verses 78 and 79 offer a powerful image of God acting in ways that move us from hopelessness to hope. Reread these verses out loud slowly. Sit quietly and prayerfully with this image. Invite God to speak to you. Share or write about whatever came to you in this time.

_____

12. How does this story offer hope to you in your time of waiting?

Ask God to fill you with hope and to speak to you of God's faithfulness, trustworthiness and purposefulness in the midst of your waiting.

Now or Later

Read Psalm 33:20-22 several times, sitting in silence for two or three minutes between readings, inviting God to open your mind and heart to whatever God has for you.

We wait in hope for the LORD;
    he is our help and our shield.
In him our hearts rejoice,
    for we trust in his holy name.
May your unfailing love rest upon us, O LORD,
    even as we put our hope in you.

Write about your experience of allowing the Spirit to use this psalm to speak to you.

6

God's Presence and Purposes in Our Waiting

Genesis 37:12-36;
39:1-23; 50:15-21

Joseph was a man who was hated and betrayed by his brothers and then later falsely accused and put in prison for seven years. Yet all the time, God was with Joseph, unfolding a greater plan.

It could not have been easy for Joseph to stay connected to the reality of God's presence with him in all he suffered, any more than it is for us in times of distress. Yet we are called to trust that God is with us, that God is good and loving, and that God is at work in ways unknown to us, bringing good even out of our times of distress.

GROUP DISCUSSION. When you think about times of waiting in the past, what made it difficult to trust that God was with you? What helped you in those times to trust that God was with you?

PERSONAL REFLECTION. Think of a time when you felt unsure of God's loving presence with you. What was the experience like for you? Now think of a time when you had a sense of God's presence with you. What happened that reassured you that God was with you?

The life story of Joseph is a story filled with heartbreak, betrayal, injustice and waiting. In this study we follow Joseph through a series of traumatic life events, any of which could have left him believing that God had abandoned him. Yet in Joseph's times of waiting for deliverance, God was with him, working to bring blessing to many. *Read Genesis 37:12-36; 39:1-23 and 50:15-21.*

---

1. What scenes stand out to you as you read through these stories from Joseph's life?

---

2. From a human point of view, what might Joseph have thought and felt about himself, other people and life in general through these experiences of betrayal and injustice?

---

3. What might he have been thinking and feeling about God?

---

4. What parts of Joseph's experiences can you relate to? Explain.

5. Some time later, Joseph was able to see God's hand at work bringing good out of what others meant for harm. How did Joseph respond to his brothers (50:15-21)?

---

6. What do you think made it possible for Joseph to respond in this way to his brothers?

---

7. What thoughts do you have about Joseph's conclusion that what others meant for harm, God intended for good?

---

8. What does this story show us about God?

---

9. In what ways have you seen God at work in times of difficult waiting?

How have those experiences (or your lack of such an experience) changed your times of waiting?

10. In what ways have your experiences of God's presence with you changed you?

---

11. How might this story of Joseph help you trust that God is present even in times of difficult waiting?

Express your gratitude to God for God's presence with you in times of waiting and always.

Now or Later

Read more of the story of Joseph in chapters 40–47 of Genesis, looking for evidence of God's plan unfolding and God's presence with him.

7

The Gifts
in Waiting

Psalm 40

We have seen that when we are going through a time of difficult waiting, on the deepest level what we are really longing and waiting for is an experience of God-with-us-as-we-wait.

When, by grace, we encounter God in our waiting, we are changed. The gifts we receive in these times of experiencing God's tender mercies toward us can have a profound and lasting impact on our awareness of God's personal love for us. This deeper trust in God's unfailing love, in turn, can strengthen us, heal us and free us in ways we might never have known otherwise.

GROUP DISCUSSION. How do you tend to express your gratitude?

PERSONAL REFLECTION. Think of a time recently when you felt grateful. What was the experience of gratitude like for you?

In this study we join the psalmist in his boundless gratitude to God for God's many kindnesses in times of waiting—kindnesses which have allowed us to experience God-with-us, loving us and caring for us. *Read Psalm 40.*

---

1. What does the psalmist say that God has done for him (vv. 1-3)?

---

2. When have you sensed that God heard your cry in a time of waiting? Explain.

---

3. What experiences have you had of God lifting you out of a slimy pit of mud and mire and giving you a firm place to stand?

---

4. What new song has God put in your heart?

---

5. What is the psalmist's response to the gifts he has received from God (vv. 4-5, 9-10)?

6. In what specific ways have you responded to the gifts God has given you in times of waiting?

---

7. In verses 6-8 the psalmist makes the statement that God does not desire religious observances (sacrifices and offerings) as an expression of our gratitude but instead wants our heart. What contrast would you draw between verbal expressions of gratitude and the kind of loving surrender (as an expression of gratitude) that is described in verses 6-8?

---

8. Why do you think the psalmist is making this point that God does not desire our religious observances but instead desires our wills and our hearts?

---

9. What would it mean to "desire to do [God's] will" and to have God's law "within [your] heart" (v. 8)? *Our attitude of obeying and serving God.*

10. What does the psalmist continue to ask for from God in verses 11-17? *Mercy*

11. What do you want to continue to ask God for at this time? *Personal sin   Quick deliverance*

Thank God for all the gifts you have received from God in your times of waiting.

Now or Later

Paraphrase verses 6-8 to make the statements more personal for you. As you are ready, pray this prayer of surrender every day as an outpouring of your love and gratitude for God's personal love and care for you.

8

The God
Who Waits

Luke 15:11-32

Waiting through difficult times can be so challenging that we might sometimes feel that the waiting itself is a form of suffering. And indeed, it can be. This is, in part, why we often experience renewed hope and strength when we are able to trust that God is with us to help us, keep us and bless us in our waiting.

We may be equally moved to learn that God knows what it is like to wait. In one of the stories that Jesus told, he described God as the waiting Father. God, our Creator, our Sustainer, our Life, waits for us.

As you study this powerful passage, may the beauty of the grace of our God speak to you in ways that allow you to truly meet God anew in your times of waiting.

GROUP DISCUSSION. What words would you use to describe an ideal relationship between a father and child?

PERSONAL REFLECTION. What words would you use to describe your relationship with your father?

The story that Jesus tells in this text is often referred to as the story of the prodigal son. But it most importantly paints a stunning portrait of God, the waiting Father, who waits for *us*, scans the horizon looking for us and runs to embrace us when we are still far from home. *Read Luke 15:11-32.*

1. What words would you use to describe the two sons in this story? *Younger son irresponsible, disrespectful, foolish, repentant Older son - bitter, stubborn, resentful,*

2. How are they different, and how are they the same?

Younger son seen as a sinner the older son represents those who work hard to please God. Younger son had a change of heart and repented humility the old son won't know,

3. In what way do you see yourself in each of them?

4. What character traits are evident in this father's waiting?

Love, compassion

5. What responses do you have to the father's waiting?

6. What did the father do when his waiting was over?

He put a robe, shoe and ring on his son's finger and threw a party

What emotions does the father's reaction stir in you?

Love

---

7. What does Jesus teach us in this story about who God is?

---

8. What does Jesus teach us in this story about how God sees us?

---

9. How does Jesus' picture of who God is compare to your images of God?

---

10. How does this story's portrayal of how God sees us compare to your ideas about how God sees you?

11. How might knowing that God is a God who waits speak to you in your times of waiting?

Thank God for being a God who waits for you with love and compassion.

Now or Later

In a time of quiet, let yourself reflect on the following images from Jesus' story:

Put yourself in this story as the son or daughter who is returning home after a time of doing things your own way. You have been longing for home, but no longer feel worthy. You have a speech planned about how unworthy you are. But suddenly, you see God, your true Father, running to meet you on the road. His arms are open, his eyes are full of joy, he calls your name with great tenderness. Let him wrap his arms around you. Listen to him say, "Welcome home, my dear child. I am overjoyed to see you. I love you."

Leader's Notes

MY GRACE IS SUFFICIENT FOR YOU. (2 COR 12:9)

Leading a Bible discussion can be an enjoyable and rewarding experience. But it can also be *scary*—especially if you've never done it before. If this is your feeling, you're in good company. When God asked Moses to lead the Israelites out of Egypt, he replied, "O Lord, please send someone else to do it!" (Ex 4:13). It was the same with Solomon, Jeremiah and Timothy, but God helped these people in spite of their weaknesses, and he will help you as well.

You don't need to be an expert on the Bible or a trained teacher to lead a Bible discussion. The idea behind these inductive studies is that the leader guides group members to discover for themselves what the Bible has to say. This method of learning will allow group members to remember much more of what is said than a lecture would.

These studies are designed to be led easily. As a matter of fact, the flow of questions through the passage from observation to interpretation to application is so natural that you may feel that the studies lead themselves. This study guide is also flexible. You can use it with a variety of groups—student, professional, neighborhood or church groups. Each study takes forty-five to sixty minutes in a group setting.

There are some important facts to know about group dynamics and encouraging discussion. The suggestions listed below should enable you to effectively and enjoyably fulfill your role as leader.

Preparing for the Study

1. Ask God to help you understand and apply the passage in your own life. Unless this happens, you will not be prepared to lead others. Pray too for the various members of the group. Ask God to open your hearts to the message of his Word and motivate you to action.

2. Read the introduction to the entire guide to get an overview of the entire book and the issues which will be explored.

3. As you begin each study, read and reread the assigned Bible passage to familiarize yourself with it.

4. This study guide is based on the New International Version of the Bible. It will help you and the group if you use this translation as the basis for your study and discussion.

5. Carefully work through each question in the study. Spend time in meditation and reflection as you consider how to respond.

6. Write your thoughts and responses in the space provided in the study guide. This will help you to express your understanding of the passage clearly.

7. It might help to have a Bible dictionary handy. Use it to look up any unfamiliar words, names or places. (For additional help on how to study a passage, see chapter five of *How to Lead a LifeGuide Bible Study*, InterVarsity Press.)

8. Consider how you can apply the Scripture to your life. Remember that the group will follow your lead in responding to the studies. They will not go any deeper than you do.

9. Once you have finished your own study of the passage, familiarize yourself with the leader's notes for the study you are leading. These are designed to help you in several ways. First, they tell you the purpose the study guide author had in mind when writing the study. Take time to think through how the study questions work together to accomplish that purpose. Second, the notes provide you with additional background information or suggestions on group dynamics for various questions. This information can be useful when people have difficulty understanding or answering a question. Third, the leader's notes can alert you to potential problems you may encounter during the study.

10. If you wish to remind yourself of anything mentioned in the leader's notes, make a note to yourself below that question in the study.

Leading the Study

1. Begin the study on time. Open with prayer, asking God to help the group to understand and apply the passage.

2. Be sure that everyone in your group has a study guide. Encourage the group to prepare beforehand for each discussion by reading the introduction to the guide and by working through the questions in the study.

3. At the beginning of your first time together, explain that these studies are meant to be discussions, not lectures. Encourage the members of the group to participate. However, do not put pressure on those who may be hesitant to speak during the first few sessions. You may want to suggest the following guidelines to your group.

☐ Stick to the topic being discussed.

☐ Your responses should be based on the verses which are the focus of the discussion and not on outside authorities such as commentaries or speakers.

☐ These studies focus on a particular passage of Scripture. Only rarely should you refer to other portions of the Bible. This allows for everyone to participate in in-depth study on equal ground.

☐ Anything said in the group is considered confidential and will not be discussed outside the group unless specific permission is given to do so.

☐ We will listen attentively to each other and provide time for each person present to talk.

☐ We will pray for each other.

4. Have a group member read the introduction at the beginning of the discussion.

5. Every session begins with a group discussion question. The question or activity is meant to be used before the passage is read. The question introduces the theme of the study and encourages group members to begin to open up. Encourage as many members as possible to participate, and be ready to get the discussion going with your own response.

This section is designed to reveal where our thoughts or feelings need to be transformed by Scripture. That is why it is especially important not to read the passage before the discussion question is asked. The passage will tend to color the honest reactions people would otherwise give because they are, of course, supposed to think the way the Bible does.

You may want to supplement the group discussion question with an icebreaker to help people to get comfortable. See the community section of *Small Group Idea Book* for more ideas.

You also might want to use the personal reflection question with your group. Either allow a time of silence for people to respond individually or discuss it together.

6. Have a group member (or members if the passage is long) read aloud the passage to be studied. Then give people several minutes to read the passage again silently so that they can take it all in.

7. Question 1 will generally be an overview question designed to briefly survey the passage. Encourage the group to look at the whole passage, but try to avoid getting sidetracked by questions or issues that will be addressed later in the study.

8. As you ask the questions, keep in mind that they are designed to be used just as they are written. You may simply read them aloud. Or you may prefer to express them in your own words.

There may be times when it is appropriate to deviate from the study guide. For example, a question may have already been answered. If so, move on to the next question. Or someone may raise an important question not covered in the guide. Take time to discuss it, but try to keep the group from going off on tangents.

9. Avoid answering your own questions. If necessary, repeat or rephrase them until they are clearly understood. Or point out something you read in the leader's notes to clarify the context or meaning. An eager group quickly becomes passive and silent if they think the leader will do most of the talking.

10. Don't be afraid of silence. People may need time to think about the question before formulating their answers.

11. Don't be content with just one answer. Ask, "What do the rest of you think?" or "Anything else?" until several people have given answers to the question.

12. Acknowledge all contributions. Try to be affirming whenever possible. Never reject an answer. If it is clearly off-base, ask, "Which verse led you to that conclusion?" or again, "What do the rest of you think?"

13. Don't expect every answer to be addressed to you, even though this will probably happen at first. As group members become more at ease, they will begin to truly interact with each other. This is one sign of healthy discussion.

14. Don't be afraid of controversy. It can be very stimulating. If you don't resolve an issue completely, don't be frustrated. Move on and keep it in mind for later. A subsequent study may solve the problem.

15. Periodically summarize what the group has said about the passage. This helps to draw together the various ideas mentioned and gives continuity to the study. But don't preach.

16. At the end of the Bible discussion you may want to allow group members a time of quiet to work on an idea under "Now or Later." Then discuss what you experienced. Or you may want to encourage group members to work on these ideas between meetings. Give an opportunity during the session for people to talk about what they are learning.

17. Conclude your time together with conversational prayer, adapting the prayer suggestion at the end of the study to your group. Ask for God's help in following through on the commitments you've made.

18. End on time.

Many more suggestions and helps are found in *How to Lead a Life-Guide Bible Study.*

Components of Small Groups

A healthy small group should do more than study the Bible. There are four components to consider as you structure your time together.

Nurture. Small groups help us to grow in our knowledge and love of God. Bible study is the key to making this happen and is the foundation of your small group.

Community. Small groups are a great place to develop deep friendships with other Christians. Allow time for informal interaction before and after each study. Plan activities and games that will help you get to know each other. Spend time having fun together going on a picnic or cooking dinner together.

Worship and prayer. Your study will be enhanced by spending time praising God together in prayer or song. Pray for each other's needs and keep track of how God is answering prayer in your group. Ask God to help you to apply what you are learning in your study.

Outreach. Reaching out to others can be a practical way of applying what you are learning, and it will keep your group from becoming self-focused. Host a series of evangelistic discussions for your friends or neighbors. Clean up the yard of an elderly friend. Serve at a soup kitchen together, or spend a day working on a Habitat house.

Many more suggestions and helps in each of these areas are found in *Small Group Idea Book.* Information on building a small group can be found in *Small Group Leaders' Handbook* and *The Big Book on Small Groups* (both from InterVarsity Press). Reading through one of these books would be worth your time.

Study 1. When Waiting Is Difficult. Psalm 13.

Purpose: To acknowledge the fears and distress that can be part of the experience of waiting, and to find hope in God's help even as we wait.

Preparation note. You may want to have pencils or pens on hand for question eleven.

Question 1. This question gives an overview of the psalm. There are no right answers in terms of titling the sections. Rather, this is an opportunity to gain a general sense about the psalm's tone and content.

Question 2. The psalmist describes having great mental and emotional distress: Mentally he is constantly wrestling with his thoughts. Emotionally he experiences sorrow every day.

Question 3. Spiritually, this time of waiting is a time of fearing that God has forgotten him. The psalmist feels abandoned by God, forgotten by God, as if he does not matter to God. He must be deeply afraid that God is gone and that he will be destroyed by his enemy.

Question 4. Encourage group members to share as freely as they desire about their mental, emotional and spiritual struggles during times of difficult waiting. Realize that everyone's experience will be different. Some people may relate closely to the psalmist's experience. Others may have had times of waiting in which, in the face of a threat or danger, they were comforted by God's presence or by a deep sense of hope. Acknowledge the validity of the range of experiences group members may have had.

Question 5. In verse 3 the psalmist pleads with God to see him and answer his call for help. He asks God to see him—to see his danger, his need, his distress—because he feels like God has forgotten him or looked away. And he asks God to answer him, to take action on his behalf, to save him from danger, because it seems God is not doing anything. He also asks God to give light to his eyes; this may be a metaphor for hope but more likely is a request for direction and help in the face of danger, direction that will allow him to defeat his enemy.

Question 6. The threat the psalmist faces is death. This is not a small threat. And it may be a threat some people in the group have faced themselves or with a loved one in the form of a life-threatening illness or some other grave danger.

Question 7. In the final section the psalmist commits to trusting God, to rejoicing in God's help before it comes and to singing to the Lord as he remembers that God has been good to him in the past. This is a huge commitment and not always an easy one to make when there is no immediate sense of God's help or presence. You might want to encourage group members to discuss the struggle involved in making a commitment like this, in this kind of situation.

Question 8. In making the commitment, the psalmist is reaffirming that God's love is unfailing, that God is a God who saves, that God is good and more specifically that God is good to each of us in response to our very personal needs.

Question 9. Encourage the group to look at each of these truths about God and reflect on them. Help them imagine the impact each truth would have on their mental, emotional and spiritual well-being in a time of difficult waiting.

Question 10. Encourage group members to allow themselves to be in any one of the phases the psalmist moves through. The passage can be a resource in helping us express our emotional, mental and spiritual distress. It can help us call out to God. And it can help us reaffirm our hope in God as it reminds us who God is.

Question 11. Allow a time of quiet for group members to pray in this way and to write about their experience. Invite them to share whatever they want to share with the group.

Study 2. Wisdom in Waiting. Proverbs 3:1-12.

Purpose: To explore the wisdom of waiting for God's guidance and correction.

Preparation note. You will need to have pencils or pens and paper on hand for questions one, nine and ten.

Question 1. The purpose of this question is to help group members be drawn into the text, as if this father were addressing them. There is no sense of accusation, disrespect or control in these verses; they are simply a record of a father clearly, lovingly sharing words of wisdom with his son.

Every member of the group should make a list as people call out answers. (They'll all need their own list for questions nine and ten.) Listing all the advice given in these twelve verses is a way of ferreting it out from the text so the group can both look at each piece of wisdom and see the list as a whole.

Question 2. Make another list, this time of the benefits of wise living. Again, creating this list helps the group see all that is being said here as well as some of the specifics regarding the benefits of wise living.

Question 4. These are two beautiful images about the central role of love and faithfulness in life. Both of these words are often used to describe God. God is loving and God is faithful. We are to love faithfully, like God loves. Love and faithfulness are foundational to all wisdom and need to guide all we are and do. We are being told to make a beautiful necklace of love and faithfulness and to wear it always. And we are being told to engrave love and faithfulness onto our hearts.

Question 5. This text exhorts us to "trust in the LORD with all [our] heart." We talk about trusting God but don't often explore the meaning of those words. You might first encourage group members to talk about the barriers to trusting God. It could be helpful to talk as well about what happens when we trust our own abilities instead: increased anxiety, for example, or attempts to control what we cannot control and the anger and frustration this leads to.

Trusting God has to do with living as if God is trustworthy. It is living in the truth that God is our Creator and that we are creatures, that God knows vastly more than we do, and that God is a good and loving God who desires what is best for us. Trusting God with all our hearts brings to mind images of our hearts at peace, resting in God's unfailing love, and images of floating on our backs in clear, cool water, or lying down in green pastures beside still waters.

We can ask God to teach us this kind of trust. We can deepen our trust by keeping gratitude lists, by remembering together what God has done for us in the past and by sharing our stories of God's activity in our lives.

Question 6. Acknowledging God in all our ways is a call to live in close relationship with and deep reliance on God. It is a call for us to invite God to guide us, correct us, help us in all that we do in life.

Questions 9-10. Give the group time to do this individual work. Let the group know that they will not be asked to share their responses to these reflections with the group unless they want to.

Questions 11-12. Encourage the group to give examples of times when wisdom might mean waiting, and explore together how realizing this truth might ease the stress of waiting. This text is about seeking God for direction, which is crucial wisdom for our times of waiting. Discuss ways this might help in times of personal waiting.

Study 3. Waiting for God. Psalm 42.

Purpose: To see more clearly what we are truly waiting for in our times of waiting.

Question 1. The psalmist uses images of a deer panting for streams of water and of his soul thirsting for God. He also uses images of the roar of waterfalls and the power of waves breaking to describe the overwhelming nature of what he is going through.

Other images include his tears being his food day and night, his bones being in mortal agony, memories of how he used to be free to worship, and his soul being downcast. The psalmist feels separated from God. This is his great agony.

Question 2. The experience of feeling separated from God is the greatest suffering we can ever experience. Built into the fabric of our being is a deep longing and need for intimacy with God. When we fear that God has abandoned us in some way, we feel hopeless. It is the experience of great darkness and dread. When we know, instead, that God is with us even in moments of feeling separated, hope is rekindled right in the midst of life's hardest challenges.

Question 3. It can be very difficult to stay conscious of such deep emotional and spiritual longing and grief, and to find words for such pain. It can also be very difficult to feel permission to acknowledge or express such deep suffering.

Question 4. Our longing for God is the deepest longing of our souls. To be aware of this longing is to open our heart and mind and soul to God in new ways, which allows our spiritual ears and eyes to become more sensitive to God's presence with us. I experienced this personally in a time of waiting during a season with cancer:

> As I waited . . . I found myself wanting to be present in the waiting. I came to see, as I waited day after day, that I was not waiting for the next event or piece of news. I was not even primarily waiting to see how God would show up at those moments in the future. Something more was happening. I was waiting for God to pour out the grace and strength I needed each day as I waited. I was waiting, watching, anticipating, opening myself up to God's presence each day as I waited. . . . I was still and quiet. My ears straining for the smallest sound. My eyes searching . . . for signs of God's presence. As I waited in this way, every day of waiting became its own gift. Some days I could feel my great thirst for God. Other days I felt joyful anticipation. And from time to time I felt God's presence so tangibly that my watching for God turned to resting with God. (Juanita Ryan, *Keep Breathing: What to Do When You Can't Figure Out What to Do* [Seattle: CreateSpace, 2009], p. 101.)

Question 5. Encourage group members to relate to the psalmist's experience in personal ways.

Question 6. People are asking "Where is your God?" and even taunting him with the question (vv. 3, 10). We read in verse 9, though, that the psalmist is also asking God, "Why have you forgotten me?" The burden of our own grief, longings and doubts may be added to by others. We can also begin to question our own reality when other people question us, mock us or accuse us in this way.

Question 7. The contrast between the experiences described in verses 3 and 4 is amazing. In verse 3, in the present tense, the psalmist is experiencing acute grief—tears have become his food day and night. In verse 4 he is remembering being a part of a festive throng, shouting in joy and thanksgiving as they marched to the house of worship.

Question 8. The psalmist reminds himself to put his hope in God, to hang on to the belief that he will again praise God who is his Savior, to remember his past experiences of God's presence in the land of Jordan and the heights of Hermon.

Question 9. You might want to give people time to write and reflect on truths that help them in times of doubt and suffering, when God seems distant.

Question 10. The psalmist is acknowledging here that he has been having some sense of God's loving, comforting, personal presence with him: "By day the Lord directs his love, at night his song is with me."

Study 4. Waiting Together. Job 2:11-13; 6:1-17; 13:1-5.
Purpose: To identify the gifts that can come as we wait together with open hearts.

Question 1. The friends responded to Job by weeping and tearing their clothes (a demonstration of shared grief) and then sat on the ground with him for seven days and seven nights without speaking a word, "because they saw how great his suffering was."

Question 2. The friends' silence spoke deeply of their compassion for Job, and of their shared grief with him. They suffered with him. They sat in humility and love with him.

Question 3. After Job's friends began to offer advice, he responded with great anguish, reminding them of his deep suffering and telling them that it's natural for such grief to lead to "impetuous words" and to "forsaking the fear of the Almighty." He also told them that they abandoned him when he needed them most, that he knows all the traditional wisdom they're spewing at him and that none of it is helpful. Moreover, he reminded them that he is not inferior to them, and asked for their devotion, understanding and respect as friends, as well as for their silence.

Question 4. In verse 6:14, Job is asking his friends to trust him and to trust God as Job cries out in anguish to God and questions God. He is not looking for pat answers; rather, he's seeking God. Job wants to talk directly with God, to pour out his questions and anger and despair and confusion.

Question 5. Silence can be better than words because our silence speaks the deepest truth—that we are powerless to take away the pain, and we don't have answers. Silence can also convey our awareness of the depth of someone's pain; it indicates that we can't think of any words that could adequately express how hard what they're going through is. Essentially, our silence communicates our presence, our "devotion" (as Job calls it), our deep respect, our compassion, our solidarity in humility with the person who is suffering.

Question 6. It is tempting to give answers to people in pain. What we often don't realize is that the reason we are tempted to do this is that it allows us to remain emotionally and spiritually distant from the pain and suffering. It allows us to push away our own questions and fears and grief in the face of another's suffering. We can appear knowledgeable, spiritual, in charge. But in doing so we are being distant, disrespectful and hurtful to the person who is suffering.

Question 7. Being on the receiving end of the gifts of true compassion and respect and silent presence can make us feel comforted, valued, loved.

Questions 8, 9 and 11. Encourage group members to make these truths personal.

Question 10. We may think that when we say all the "right" things like Job's friends tried to do that we are somehow representing God. But the opposite is true. When we offer ourselves—our compassionate hearts, our shared presence in humility and respect—we are being the presence of Christ. It is a presence that offers strength and comfort to the person who is suffering, because it will alleviate the greatest suffering of all—the fear that we are all alone in our pain.

Study 5. Waiting with Hope. Luke 1:1-25, 57-80.
Purpose: To explore the possibility of finding hope even as we wait.
Question 1. The purpose of this question is to help the group gain an overview of these two sections of the first chapter of Luke's gospel.
Question 2. Encourage group members to name the things that matter a great deal to them that they have waited a long time for.
Question 3. Zechariah must have felt a strange mixture of fear, awe, amazement and doubt.
Question 4. The sign of temporarily not being able to speak could have been a gift in many ways. Sometimes the practice of silence allows us to hear others and God in new ways. Our eyes and ears and hearts and minds can become more receptive. The sign of muteness was also a sign to all who heard this story. It immediately alerted the crowd outside the temple that something had happened. In addition, it alerted the crowd on the day of John's circumcision that God was doing something very significant.
Questions 7-8. Encourage group members to take the time for personal reflection about God's activity in their lives.
Question 9. Reading this text from the perspective of God as the main Actor gives a very different sense of the story. It is not so much about the humans who are full of fears and uncertainties as it is about a God whose love is active and powerful in our lives and in this world.
Question 10. Reading the text from the perspective of God as the main Actor can bring a sense of peace and hope. We do not have to figure things out and make things happen. It is God who acts, God who saves, God who transforms. It is God who causes the sun to shine on those living in darkness.
Question 11. Allow the group to sit with these powerful images for a few minutes after you read the verses. Give them time to write about their reflections and to share whatever they choose to share with the group.

Study 6. God's Presence and Purposes in Our Waiting. Genesis 37:12-36; 39:1-23; 50:15-21.
Purpose: To deepen our awareness of God's presence with us and purposes in our times of waiting.

Question 1. The purpose of this question is to help the group gain an overview of the major events of Joseph's life during this time period. **Question 2.** Joseph had to have been deeply traumatized by the violence, the betrayals, the envy, the abuse of power, the lies that were a part of these tragic events. He may have lost hope in any sense of justice, any sense of protection from others. It must have seemed that evil was more powerful than good. **Question 3.** Joseph very likely felt abandoned by God, and maybe even punished by God. He may also have despaired of being protected or helped or vindicated by God. **Question 4.** Encourage group members to share as personally as they feel free to. **Question 6.** Joseph seems to have been able to stay in a place of deep humility before God in spite of the powerful position God had placed him in. He may have had moments of sensing God's presence with him through his great suffering, and he certainly was able to look back over the arc of his life and see how God had used his suffering to bring much good to many. **Question 7.** Sometimes, when we have lived through a time of difficulty, we are able, like Joseph, to see how God was active in our times of struggle, bringing good out of our suffering. Invite group members to share personal stories of this kind of experience in their own lives. **Question 8.** When we are abused, betrayed, treated as "less than," falsely accused or treated unjustly, it can seem that evil is more powerful than good. We are likely to become spiritually discouraged and maybe even despair. We will probably question ourselves and God. We may feel that we are somehow to blame, or that we have been rejected or abandoned by God.

But the story of Joseph shows us clearly that God never leaves us. It is clear that God's hand of care and provision and presence were with Joseph. All the time that others were lying and falsely accusing and being violent toward Joseph, God was blessing him and allowing Joseph to be a blessing to others. It is a story of God's power and love and presence in all circumstances. **Question 9.** Encourage group members to share as much as they are comfortable sharing of the ways they have struggled to know God's presence with them while waiting, and the ways they have been aware of God with them.

Study 7. The Gifts in Waiting. Psalm 40.

Purpose: To acknowledge and praise God for the ways God comes to us, responds to us, delivers us.

Question 1. The psalmist talks about waiting patiently for the Lord, and experiencing God's eventual response. God "turned to [him] and heard [his] cry," the psalmist wrote. And God acted. God "lifted [him] out of the slimy pit, out of the mud and mire," and set him on solid rock. And then God "put a new song in [his] mouth," a song of praise to God for this deliverance, this help.

Questions 2-4. Encourage group members to reflect in personal ways on this text. It may be that some people are still feeling that they are in the mud and mire. Their experience may be that they are continuing to call to God for help and are still waiting for any sign of a response. Encourage this level of honesty. Clearly, the psalmist waited. And perhaps not always patiently.

Others may be able to share a time in the distant or recent past when they experienced God's healing or rescue or help in some way. Invite them to share, knowing that these kinds of events are sacred treasures and deserve to be honored. Thank each one for what they share.

Question 5. The psalmist talks in an open, intimate way in verses 4 and 5 to God, who has helped him in very personal ways, thanking God for who God is and what God has done for him. Then in verses 9 and 10 the psalmist continues with his new song of thanksgiving to God by sharing his story with others; he speaks of God's faithfulness, righteousness, salvation, love and truth to others.

Question 7. The phrase "my ears you have pierced" refers to the action taken when a servant was free to leave his master's service but chose of his own free will to stay with his master. It parallels the phrase "I desire to do your will, O my God."

When we experience God's powerful, intimate, personal interventions of grace in our lives, we respond on many levels. The expression of gratitude to God directly is one response. The sharing of our story of God's love is another. And the giving of our lives, our wills, to the God who made us and loved us is the ultimate, full expression of our response of love to God's amazing love.

Question 8. The psalmist has had a personal encounter with the true and living God. He has experienced personal love and care, personal healing and help. He has come to understand that what God desires is relationship with us. This does not mean that religious observances don't have a place but rather that they are not an end in themselves. Sometimes when we see God as frightening, harsh, impossible to please or one who abandons us, we use religious observances in an attempt to placate God. The psalmist has encountered Love and is responding in love, giving his will and his heart to God in joyful gratitude.

Question 9. These phrases about desiring to do God's will and having God's law in our hearts echo the text in Proverbs 3 that we explored in the second study. They reflect a central theme in all of Scripture: we are called to live in close, loving relationship with God, relying on our Maker for wisdom and guidance and help in all circumstances.

Question 10. The psalmist continues to cry out to God. He continues to be aware of his need for God's help on a daily basis and thus to rely and call on God who is his help and deliverer.

Study 8. The God Who Waits. Luke 15:11-32.

Purpose: To find strength and comfort in the God who waits in love for us.

Question 1. The younger son could be described by words like *irresponsible, disrespectful, foolish, repentant.* For the older son, words like *dutiful, bitter, stubborn* and *resentful* might be used.

Question 2. There are some obvious differences between the two sons. The son who is the prodigal represents those who do not follow the rules, who are seen by others as sinners. The older son, who stays home and obeys his father and slaves away for him, represents those who work hard to please God, to be good, to "get it right." Another difference between them is that the prodigal son seems to have a change of heart and come to a place of repentance (or at least humility), but we don't know if the older son repents from his bitterness and accepts the father's love.

If we look deeper, we can also see many ways that they are the same. They both turn their back on their father at some point. The prodigal does so out of selfish interests to seek pleasure. The older son does so in self-righteous anger, seeking approval; in this way he too is focused on his own selfish interests. Most significant of all is that both sons miss the deepest truth: that they are children of their father. They are not servants or slaves. They do not have to earn their father's love or approval. They are precious children whom the father sees as deeply worthy of the love he has for them both. This is why the father does not listen to the younger son's speech about being unworthy but instead treats him as royalty. And it's the reason why the father corrects the older son when he complains about always slaving for his father; he calls him what he is, "My son," and reminds him that everything he has is his.

Question 4. The fact that the father saw the son when he was a long way off and ran to him shows us that the father was waiting with longing for his son's return, with hope that his son would return, and with great love and compassion for his son. There is not a hint of anger, frustration, impatience, condemnation or any other negative reaction on the father's part. The son is prepared for shaming and judgment and is prepared to beg for a job as a servant in his father's house. But he receives a robe and ring, an embrace and blessings and a celebration in his honor instead.

Question 6. When the father's waiting was over, he ran a long way toward his son, he embraced his son and kissed him, he put a robe, shoes and a ring on him, and he threw a party!

Question 7. When we have walked away from God to live according to our self-will, God waits in love and longing for us, calling us home, eager to embrace us. We see here God who is patient, God who is forgiving, God who is openly affectionate and emotional, God who is full of longing, joy and self-giving love.

Question 8. This story has vital truths for us. God sees us very differently than we tend to see ourselves. God sees us through eyes of love and compassion. We are valued beyond measure. We are loved always. We cannot earn this value or this love because they are already ours and always will be ours. We are God's deeply loved children, in whom God delights. We are embraced, celebrated, called God's own children.

Questions 9-11. Encourage group members to share personally about the ways this story contrasts and compares with their sense of who God is and their sense of how God sees them. Help them reflect in personal ways about what it means to them that God is a God who waits for us with compassion and longing.

Juanita Ryan is a clinical nurse specialist with an M.S.N. in psychiatric mental health nursing, which she has taught at Bethel University, Rio Hondo Community College and Biola University. She has been a therapist in private practice at Brea Family Counseling Center in Brea, California, for the past two decades. She is the coauthor of The Twelve Steps: A Spiritual Kindergarten, Rooted in God's Love *and* Soul Repair, *the author of* Keep Breathing: What to Do When You Can't Figure Out What to Do *and* An Enduring Embrace: Experiencing the Love at the Heart of Prayer, *and the author or coauthor of over thirty InterVarsity Press Bible studies. She writes a blog,* Graceful Growth, *at juanitaryan.com.*

What should we study next?

We have LifeGuides for . . .

Knowing Jesus
Advent of the Savior
Following Jesus
I Am
Abiding in Christ
Jesus' Final Week

Knowing God
Meeting God
God's Comfort
God's Love
The 23rd Psalm
Miracles
Distorted Images of God

Growing in the Spirit
Meeting the Spirit
Fruit of the Spirit
Spiritual Gifts
Spiritual Warfare

Looking at the Trinity
Images of Christ
Images of God
Images of the Spirit

Developing Disciplines
Christian Disciplines
God's Word
Hospitality
The Lord's Prayer
Prayer
Praying the Psalms
Sabbath
Worship

Deepening Your Doctrine
Angels
Christian Beliefs
The Cross
End Times
Good & Evil
Heaven
The Kingdom of God
The Story of Scripture

Seekers
Encountering Jesus
Jesus the Reason
Meeting Jesus

Leaders
Christian Leadership
Integrity
Elijah
Joseph

Shaping Your Character
Christian Character
Decisions
Self-Esteem
Parables
Pleasing God
Woman of God
Women of the New Testament
Women of the Old Testament

Living Fully at Every Stage
Singleness
Marriage
Parenting
Couples of the Old Testament
Couples of the New Testament
Growing Older & Wiser

Reaching Our World
Missions
Evangelism
Four Great Loves
Loving Justice

Living Your Faith
Christian Virtues
Forgiveness

Growing in Relationships
Christian Community
Friendship